EXPLORING • SPACE

The Shuttle

David Baker
and Heather Kissock

United States

Atlantis

WEIGL PUBLISHERS INC.

Published by Weigl Publishers Inc.
350 5th Avenue, Suite 3304, PMB 6G
New York, NY 10118-0069

Website: www.weigl.com

Library of Congress Cataloging-in-Publication Data available upon request.
Fax 1-866-44-WEIGL for the attention of the Publishing Records department.

ISBN 978-1-59036-767-4 (hard cover)
ISBN 978-1-59036-768-1 (soft cover)

Printed in the United States of America
2 3 4 5 6 7 8 9 0 12 11 10 09

Weigl would like to acknowledge Getty Images and NASA as its primary photo suppliers for this title.

Every reasonable effort has been made to trace ownership and to obtain permission to reprint copyright material. The publishers would be pleased to have any errors or omissions brought to their attention so that they may be corrected in subsequent printings.

EDITOR: Heather Kissock
DESIGN: Terry Paulhus

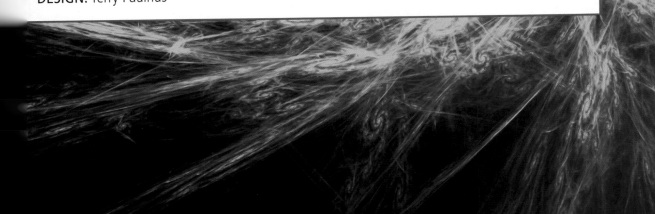

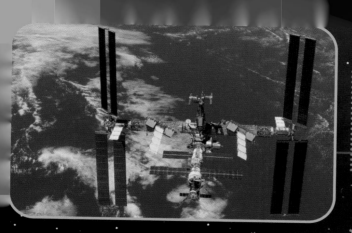

One of the space shuttle's main responsibilities is transporting scientists to the International Space Station.

The space shuttle is the world's first reusable spacecraft. By landing like an airplane, its parts are preserved, allowing it to be sent into space more than once.

Space shuttle astronauts undergo a great deal of training before they can fly into space.

BRAIN BOOSTER

The shuttle weighs almost 2,300 tons (2,337 tonnes) It can carry more than 25 tons (25.5 t) of cargo and up to seven people into orbit.

The shuttle can travel at more than 17,000 miles (27,360 kilometers) per hour. It can reach this speed in about eight minutes.

When in space, the shuttle orbits about 200 miles (322 km) from Earth's surface.

Shuttle
Showcase

The shuttle is made up of three separate sections. These are the orbiter, the external tank, and two solid rocket boosters.

1 ORBITER
The orbiter is the place where the crew live and work. It has a big bay for carrying cargo into space. The orbiter has three main engines for reaching orbit and wings for returning safely back down through the **atmosphere**.

2 EXTERNAL TANK
The external tank carries 528,000 gallons (2 million liters) of liquid hydrogen and liquid oxygen as fuel for the three engines in the orbiter.

3 ROCKET BOOSTERS
The rocket boosters help push the orbiter and the external tank along for the first two minutes of flight. The boosters weigh about 650 tons (660 t).

Shuttle Specs

Length
Space Shuttle: 184.2 feet
(56.14 meters)
Orbiter: 122.17 feet (37.24 m)

Orbiter Height
56.67 feet (17.27 m)

Wingspan
78.06 feet (23.79 m)

Weight
At liftoff: 4.5 million pounds
(2 million kilograms)
At landing: 230,000 pounds
(104,326 kg)

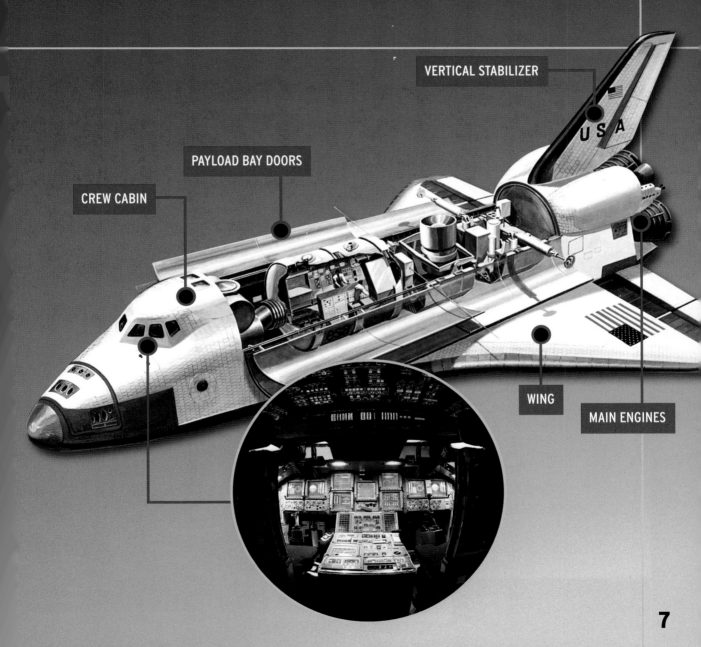

VERTICAL STABILIZER

USA

PAYLOAD BAY DOORS

CREW CABIN

WING

MAIN ENGINES

Designing
the Shuttle

Before the shuttle was made, people had to rely on different types of machinery to send things into space. Most of this machinery could only be used once and was very expensive to build. In order to save money and make space travel easier, the U.S. government asked some of its space engineers to design a new type of machine that could be used over and over again.

NASA's engineers immediately thought of a spaceship that could run like an airplane. At first, they wanted to build two vehicles. One vehicle, the orbiter, would be carried on the back of the other vehicle, known as the booster. The booster would have enough power to carry the orbiter to a great height. Once the two vehicles were far enough from Earth, the orbiter would separate from the booster and continue its journey into space. The booster would return to Earth and land like an aircraft.

Before the space shuttle was created, people were sent into space using rockets.

When this plan was reviewed by NASA, however, it was determined to cost too much to put in place. After more talking and planning, the engineers decided not to use a winged booster. They would use two solid **propellant** boosters that could be lowered back down to the ocean on parachutes instead. The boosters would be brought ashore by special recovery ships. They could then be cleaned out, refilled, and used again on future missions. These boosters would cost less to make than the winged boosters.

NASA scientists constantly look for ways to improve the shuttle.

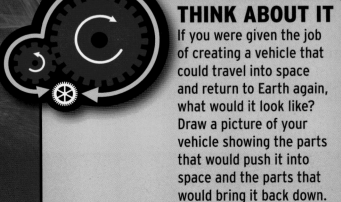

THINK ABOUT IT

If you were given the job of creating a vehicle that could travel into space and return to Earth again, what would it look like? Draw a picture of your vehicle showing the parts that would push it into space and the parts that would bring it back down.

At Home in Space

While in space, astronauts live and work inside the orbiter. Most of their time is spent in the crew cabin, located at the front of the orbiter. The crew cabin is divided into an upper and a lower area. The upper section is used for controlling the shuttle. This is where the pilots and other shuttle technicians work. The lower section contains the crew's living quarters. The galley, or kitchen, bedrooms, and washroom are found in this part of the orbiter. A storage area for exercise equipment, experiments, and personal items also is found in this lower section.

The rear section of the orbiter contains the payload bay. This is where equipment and machinery, such as satellites, are kept until they are put into space. The payload bay is 60 feet (18.2 m) long and 15 feet (4.6 m) in **diameter**. Objects are moved in and out of the payload bay using a robot called the remote manipulator arm. The arm is controlled by a technician sitting in the crew cabin.

When in space, the payload doors are kept open. This helps regulate the temperature inside the shuttle.

Surviving In Space

Living in space requires special **adaptations**. There is no air in space, so astronauts must breathe air that is carried inside the orbiter. It is stored in special tanks at the bottom of the payload bay. The tanks hold enough air for about three weeks.

In orbit, outside temperatures are more than 250° Fahrenheit (120° Celsius) in the sunlight and −240°F (−150°C) at night. Inside, the shuttle is kept at a constant 70°F (20°C) for comfort. To keep the astronauts warm and provide them with light, the shuttle must be able to produce power. Electrical power for lighting and equipment comes from **fuel cells**. Fuel cells make water, which is placed inside radiators to cool the crew compartment. After the water has been cleaned by special filters, the crew also use it for drinking.

When inside the shuttle, astronauts dress as they would on Earth. If going for a spacewalk, however, they must wear a spacesuit. The spacesuit has many features that help astronauts survive the outside environment of space.

The External Tank

The external tank is the biggest part of the shuttle. It carries the orbiter as it travels to space. The external tank holds the fuels the orbiter burns in its engines. Inside the tank, there are two sections. One is for liquid oxygen and the other for liquid hydrogen. When the hydrogen burns, it expands and is released as exhaust from a nozzle at the back of each engine. The exhaust propels the shuttle into space.

The external tank is made of a lightweight metal. It is 154 feet (46.9 m) long and 27.6 feet (8.5 m) in diameter. When empty, it weighs only 33 tons (33.5 t). Full of fuel, however, it weighs 800 tons (813 t). Each second, the orbiter's three main engines burn 1,100 gallons (4,164 L) of hydrogen and oxygen. If that were gasoline, it would be enough to drive a small car twice round the world.

The external tanks are made in Louisiana. They are transported to the Kennedy Space Center in Florida by barge.

All of the fuel is burnt in just eight minutes. At that point, the shuttle's engines shut down, and the external tank breaks away from the shuttle. It begins its descent back to Earth. When the external tank enters the atmosphere, parts of it burn up, while the rest of it drops into the ocean. These pieces are the only part of the space shuttle to not be reused.

The external tank falls into the ocean about one hour after the shuttle's launch.

GET CONNECTED

More details about the shuttle's parts, including the external tank, can be found at http://space flight.nasa.gov/shuttle/reference/shutref/et/.

Solid Rocket
Boosters

Rocket boosters give the orbiter and external tank an extra push off the launch pad. Each booster is a hollow steel case packed with solid fuel. The fuel in each booster weighs about 1.1 million pounds (453,600 kg). The boosters themselves weigh 193,000 pounds (87,543 kg) without fuel.

When ignited, or lit, the booster fuel begins to burn from top to bottom. The force of this burning produces 3,000 tons (3,048 t) of **thrust**. This is more power than 32 Boeing 747 jets give when taking off at the same time. The force pushes the shuttle upward into the air. Without the boosters, the shuttle would not leave the launch pad.

The solid rocket boosters are used in matched pairs. They both receive their fuel at the same time from the same batch. This ensures that they will perform with similar levels of thrust when launched.

The boosters burn most of their fuel in the first two minutes. By that time, the shuttle is about 28 miles (45 km) aboveground. While the shuttle continues to climb, the boosters separate from it. At this point, the orbiter's three engines push the shuttle into space, and the rocket boosters begin their return to Earth. Three giant parachutes gently lower each booster to a splashdown in the Atlantic Ocean. Here, they are recovered and used again to launch another shuttle mission.

Each solid rocket booster contains its own motor, electronics system, and recovery beacon.

BRAIN BOOSTER

To make a booster reusable, it must be taken apart and cleaned.

Each booster is made up of segments, or cylinders, that stack on top of each other. These segments are filled with a mix of the fuel and the **oxygen** needed to make them burn.

Liftoff

To prepare the shuttle for launch, its pieces must be put together. This is done in NASA's Vehicle Assembly Building, about 3 miles (4.8 km) from the launch pad at the Kennedy Space Center in Florida. The two solid rocket boosters are built on a special platform inside the building. Then, the external tank is set between the boosters and bolted into place. The orbiter is lifted by hoist and attached to the external tank. Once the shuttle is ready to travel to the launch pad, it is carried out by a giant machine called a crawler-transporter.

The shuttle usually spends about three weeks at the pad. During this time, it is prepared for the mission. Cargo, satellites, or spacecraft are put into the payload bay. Computers and electrical systems are updated and tested. Fuel is added to the shuttle's external tank. A full practice-run of the launch is held during this time as well.

Shortly after liftoff, the shuttle will roll over so that the orbiter is underneath the external tank and solid rocket boosters. It heads into space in this position.

On the day of the launch, an inspection team heads out to the launch pad for one last review of the shuttle. Another team checks the shuttle's systems to make sure they are ready. When everything is approved, the astronauts enter the orbiter. Once inside, the astronauts run a few more system checks with **Ground Control**, and all other workers leave the area.

Once the shuttle and the astronauts are ready, the countdown to the launch begins. **Ignition** comes six seconds before zero in the countdown. At this time, the three main engines on the orbiter fire. Computers check that everything is working as it should. When the counter reaches zero, the two boosters ignite, and the shuttle lifts off the pad.

The shuttle launches in an upright position.

THINK ABOUT IT The astronauts are allowed to take personal items on board the shuttle. They are loaded onto the shuttle the day before lift-off. What kinds of things do you think they take with them? What items would you take if you were heading into space? Why would you choose these items?

The Shuttle's Role in Space

The shuttle was designed to carry people and cargo to and from space. In the past, the shuttle also was used for experiments. Now, experiments are done on the International Space Station, and the space shuttle is used to take astronauts to the station.

Satellites make up most of the shuttle's cargo. There are many types of satellite. Astronomy satellites take pictures of space. Communications satellites transfer signals so that people can talk on telephones, watch television, and listen to the radio. Weather satellites keep track of weather systems moving around Earth. They help **meteorologists** predict future weather patterns.

Along with several other countries, the United States is using the shuttle to build the giant International Space Station in Earth's orbit. The shuttle carries heavy **modules** in its cargo bay, and its remote manipulator arm lifts them out. Astronauts take spacewalks to do the assembly work needed to build the space station. When built, the space station will help scientists learn more about space.

The shuttle has played a key role in building the International Space Station. It has carried many of the station's components to the site.

An Arm Up
In Space

The remote manipulator arm is sometimes called the Canadarm. This is because it was invented and built by the Canadian Space Agency.

Carrying satellites and other equipment into space is only one of the space shuttle's jobs. It also has to unload this cargo from its payload bay and deposit it into space. Moving this equipment to and from the shuttle requires technology that can be gentle, yet powerful. The remote manipulator arm was designed to be both.

The arm is about 50 feet (15 m) long and is anchored inside the shuttle's payload bay. It is controlled by astronauts from inside the shuttle. Like a human arm, the shuttle's arm can bend at its shoulder, elbow, and wrist. Attached to the wrist is a hand that is used to grasp and hold onto equipment. The arm weighs less than 1,000 pounds (45 kg), but in space, it can lift more than 586,000 pounds (266,000 kg).

Helping Us on Earth

In recent years, the space shuttle has been used to launch satellites into space as well as take scientists to the International Space Station. When the shuttle was first created, however, it was the center of many of the studies and experiments that took place in space.

Some experiments have focused on examining the planets and other objects in space. While working on the space shuttle, scientists have studied and measured the Sun's **corona**. They also have collected data on the speed of solar winds. This has helped them understand what happens on the Sun and how it affects Earth.

The corona extends more than 620,000 miles (1,000,000 km) from the Sun's surface.

GET CONNECTED

What other changes take place in a human body when it goes into space? Go to http://education. jsc.nasa.gov/explorers/p3.html to find out more.

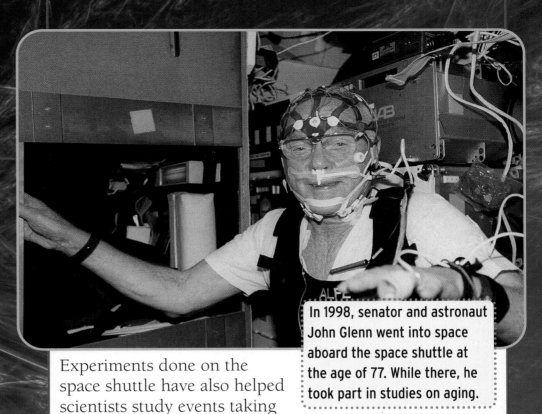

Experiments done on the space shuttle have also helped scientists study events taking place on Earth. On some missions, scientists study Earth's climate. One experiment, the Lidar In-space Technology Experiment (LITE), used laser pulses to record data on storms, pollution, and forest fires. This information helps scientists learn about the effects of climate change on Earth. The data is used by scientists to improve the quality of life on Earth.

Space is a great place for scientists to learn more about the human body. When astronauts travel into space, their bodies change. They begin to show signs of aging. Muscles waste away and become weak. Bones lose calcium and become fragile. The heart slows down and is less effective at pumping blood. Studies carried out on astronauts in space let scientists study how **microgravity** and the high **radiation** levels found in space lead to symptoms of aging. This allows doctors to better understand what happens to the body when people age. They can then come up with ways to reduce the effects of aging.

Making
the Grade

Working on the space shuttle requires people to have very specific skills, education, and **personality traits**. Astronauts must be able to perform specific tasks, work well with others, and stay calm under pressure. It takes years of experience and education to achieve the skills needed to be a space shuttle astronaut. Once these skills are mastered, there are three areas in which space shuttle astronauts can specialize.

PILOT ASTRONAUT

A pilot astronaut guides the space shuttle into space, steers it through space, and brings it back down to Earth. There are normally two pilots on the space shuttle. The commander pilot is responsible for the safety of the crew, payload, and shuttle, as well as the success of the mission. The pilot assists the commander in operating the shuttle. He or she may operate the remote manipulator arm to move satellites and other cargo.

ASTRONAUT QUALIFICATIONS

CITIZENSHIP

Pilots and mission specialists must be U.S. citizens. Payload specialists can be from other countries.

EDUCATION

Astronauts must have a minimum bachelor's degree in engineering, biology, physics, or mathematics. Most astronauts have a **doctorate**.

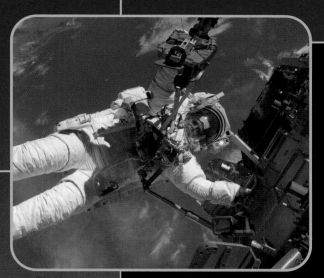

MISSION SPECIALIST

A mission specialist's main job is to do specific tasks related to the shuttle's mission. Mission specialists may work with the payload, perform experiments, or operate the remote manipulator arm. They will have expert knowledge on the systems that make the shuttle run and how to use these to do their jobs. There will be three to five mission specialists on any space shuttle flight.

PAYLOAD SPECIALIST

The payload specialist works with the cargo or experiment the shuttle is taking into space. Payload specialists have specific knowledge about the payload and know what needs to be done with it when it reaches space. These astronauts are not always NASA employees. They often are hired by the companies or countries who own the payload. They still must meet NASA's astronaut requirements before they can fly on the shuttle.

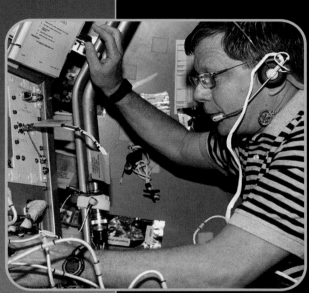

EXPERIENCE

Astronauts must have at least three years of experience in a science-related field. Pilots must have jet experience with more than 1,000 hours of in-command flight time.

HEALTH

All astronauts must pass a NASA physical, with specific vision and blood pressure requirements.

HEIGHT

Pilots must be 64 to 76 inches (162.5 to 193 cm) tall. Mission or payload specialists must be 58.5 to 76 inches (148.5 to 193 cm) tall.

A Day in Space

A day in space usually has a set schedule, with certain tasks to be done at specific times. Flight controllers on Earth wake up the crew in the morning with a pop song that they blast over the shuttle's speakers. For breakfast, astronauts eat a meal that they chose before launch. Each meal is labelled with the astronaut's name and the day it should be eaten. After eating, it is time for the astronauts to get ready for work.

A list, known as the flight plan, tells the crew what they are to work on each day. Sometimes, there is the need for a spacewalk. Other times, the crew carries out housekeeping duties, such as trash collection and cleaning. Breaks, such as lunch and dinner, are scheduled throughout the day. Keeping fit in such a small space is very important. Blocks of time are put aside for the astronauts to set up and use exercise equipment. At the end of the work day, the astronauts may read a book or listen to music.

Teamwork is an essential part of space shuttle life. Astronauts live in a confined space for days. They must all work together to make the trip comfortable for everyone on board.

The Daily Schedule

8:30 to 10:00 a.m.: Post-sleep (Morning station inspection, breakfast, morning **hygiene**)

10:00 to 10:30 a.m.: Planning and coordination (Daily planning conference and status report)

10:30 a.m. to 1:00 p.m.: Exercise (Set-up exercise equipment, exercise, and put equipment away)

1:00 to 2:00 p.m.: Lunch, personal hygiene

2:00 to 3:30 p.m.: Daily systems operations (Work preparation, report writing, emails, to-do list review, trash collection)

3:30 to 10:00 p.m.: Work (Work set-up and maintenance, performing experiments and payload operations, checking positioning and operating systems)

10:00 p.m. to 12:00 a.m.: Pre-sleep (food preparation, evening meal, and hygiene)

12:00 to 8:30 a.m.: Sleep

The work that astronauts do on the shuttle is serious, but there is always time to enjoy the experience of being in space.

Landing

At the end of a mission, the astronauts prepare for their return to Earth. They pack away all the equipment they have used while in orbit. They also put away any items that can get thrown around when the shuttle re-enters Earth's atmosphere. Packing often takes a full day.

During landing preparations, the astronauts put on their launch and landing suits. These suits are specially designed to handle emergency situations that may occur as the shuttle lands or lifts off.

BRAIN BOOSTER

If weather conditions are poor in Florida, the space shuttle lands at Edwards Air Force Base in California. It is then transported back to the Kennedy Space Center on the back of a 747 jetliner.

When entering the Earth's atmosphere, the shuttle encounters many poisonous gases that can remain on the shuttle even after it lands. As a result, the space shuttle has to sit on the runway for about 20 minutes after it lands. This is the amount of time it takes for the gases to blow away.

There are more than 30,000 tiles on the outside of the orbiter. Without these tiles, the orbiter would burn up when it enters Earth's atmosphere.

While the crew prepares for landing, the pilots guide the shuttle back to Earth. As the orbiter slowly comes toward the atmosphere, Earth's gravity increases the shuttle's speed to almost 18,000 miles (28,968 km) per hour. Then, as the shuttle enters the atmosphere, **friction** begins to slow it down again. As it slows, the friction heats up the shuttle. Special **insulating** tiles, each about the size of a human hand, absorb this heat.

The shuttle begins its glide back to Earth almost halfway around the globe from its landing site. Typically, the shuttle lands at the Kennedy Space Center in Florida. For a landing here, the shuttle begins to slow down over the central Pacific Ocean. The speed of the orbiter is reduced using small rockets as braking motors. It begins to descend along a pre-determined path.

As the orbiter glides toward the runway, the pilots guide it in "s"-shaped curves to slow its speed further. The pilots watch to see if the orbiter is in the correct position for landing. When it is lined up perfectly with the landing strip, the orbiter is brought down to the runway. As it rolls down the runway, a parachute pops out behind the orbiter, helping it come to a complete stop.

Test Your
Knowledge

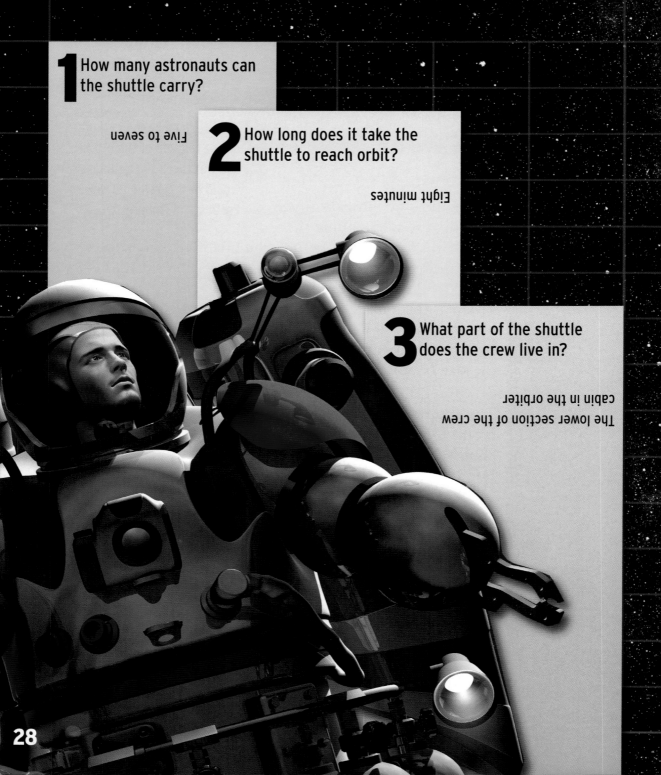

1 How many astronauts can the shuttle carry?

Five to seven

2 How long does it take the shuttle to reach orbit?

Eight minutes

3 What part of the shuttle does the crew live in?

The lower section of the crew cabin in the orbiter

4 What is the biggest part of the shuttle?

External tank

5 What do the rocket boosters do?

Give the orbiter and external tanks an extra push off the launch pad

6 Where is the shuttle put together?

NASA's Vehicle Assembly Building at the Kennedy Space Center in Florida

7 What is another name for the orbiter's remote manipulator arm?

Canadarm

8 What is a flight plan?

A list that contains the astronauts' daily schedule

9 Name three types of astronaut that work on the shuttle.

Pilot astronauts, mission specialists, and payload specialists

10 Why does the shuttle sit on the runway for 20 minutes after landing?

To let poisonous gases blow away

Further
Resources

How can I find out more about the space shuttle?
Most libraries have computers that connect to a database for researching information. If you input a key word, you will be provided with a list of books in the library that contain information on that topic. Non-fiction books are arranged numerically, using their call number. Fiction books are organized alphabetically by the author's last name.

Websites

To get the latest info on the space shuttles and their missions, go to **www.nasa.gov/centers/kennedy/shuttle operations/index.html**.

Important dates in space shuttle history can be found at **www.infoplease.com/spot/ spaceshuttletimeline.html**.

Practice launching the shuttle using the simulator found at **www.pao.ksc.nasa.gov/ sim/index2.html**.

WWW.PAO.KSC.NASA.GOV/SIM/INDEX2.HTML

Glossary

adaptations: changes made to fit into an environment

atmosphere: the layer of gases that surrounds Earth

boosters: rockets that give the shuttle an extra push off the launch pad

corona: a layer of gas that surrounds the Sun

diameter: the length of a line that extends to both sides of a circle

doctorate: an advanced university degree

friction: the conversion of energy into heat as one material moves against another

fuel cells: devices that produce power by changing fuel and oxygen into heat and electricity

Ground Control: the place on Earth that stays in constant contact with the shuttle astronauts in space

hygiene: the process of keeping clean

ignition: the process of starting an engine

insulating: covering something with a material that slows or stops the flow of electricity, heat, or sound

meteorologists: scientists who study Earth's atmosphere to forecast weather

microgravity: a state in which the force of gravity is so weak that weightlessness occurs

modules: parts of spacecraft that have special uses and can be separated from the rest of the craft

NASA: National Aeronautics and Space Administration, the United States' civilian agency for research into space and aviation

orbit: to move in a path around a planet or other space object

personality traits: behaviors that make a person distinct

propellant: a substance that is used to push something forward

radiation: energy given off in the form of waves or very tiny particles

satellite: a spacecraft that moves in orbit around Earth, the Moon, or other bodies in space for a specific purpose

space station: a spacecraft that orbits around Earth like a satellite, but can house people for long periods of time

thrust: the force that occurs when an object is pushed

Index